Drip ... drop ... drip ... drop. Raindrops fell on the roof of the kennel.

Kevin and Wellington were sitting in the kennel. They were waiting for the rain to stop.

The raindrops got bigger.

Splish ... splash ... splosh.

The rain went into the kennel.

Then the sky went black. There was a flash, ... then a crash, ... bang! Kevin was afraid.

Big raindrops went into the kennel. Soon there was a big puddle. Kevin was afraid.

Flash ... crash ... bang! Flash ... crash ... bang! Kevin hid behind Wellington. He was afraid.

The water was getting deep.

It reached Kevin's tail.

"Help … help," cried Kevin.

"I am afraid."

He began to splash about in the kennel. Soon he was swimming in the rain with Wellington.

The two dogs swam to a grassy bank. They waited for the rain to stop.

Drip … drop …drip …drop. The rain stopped. There was a rainbow in the sky. Kevin felt happy again.

"ai"

rain

raindrops

waiting

afraid

tail

rainbow

High Frequency Words

on the of and in they for to went was a he it dogs I am at big getting

were got then there water about with two help again